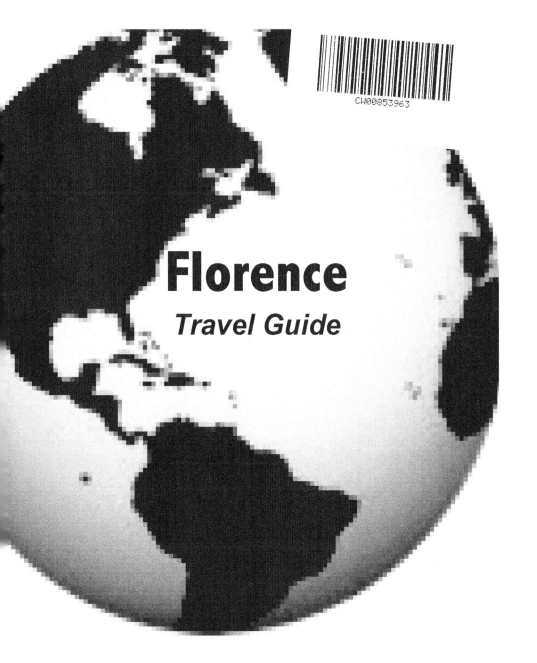

Florence
Travel Guide

Quick Trips Series

Table of Contents

KNOW BEFORE YOU GO 51

Florence

Florence (Firenze) is Tuscany's capital and was once

Italy's capital. The city is known for its influence during the

Renaissance period between the 14th and 17th centuries.

Florence has stunning artwork and galleries, manicured

gardens, winding streets and delightful waterfront shops.

FLORENCE TRAVEL GUIDE

The Renaissance (meaning 'rebirth' in French) was a cultural movement which spread across Europe and resulted in the rebirth of education, teaching and learning in its many forms.

As one of the most visited cities in Europe during the past 1000 years, Florence charms its way into the visitor's heart like no other.

In sciences, Leonardo da Vinci spearheaded the study of the human anatomy, while Galileo revealed that the Earth revolved around the Sun. In politics ancient texts untouched for over 1000 years were uncovered and debated, while most notably, the arts took a new life form of their own.

Fundamental new techniques were imposed, and artists learned how to paint and sketch in three dimensions, bringing more life, drama and emotion to their works. In architecture, buildings were bigger and grander than ever, taking into account new rules on proportion and taking inspiration from the classical past. All of this in turn influenced painting, sculpture and architecture of the highest calibre.

Although modern day Florence may be a little different, its greatest attraction is the fact that these inspiring paintings, faultless sculptures and seamless architecture still remain today. Away from the city, some of Tuscany's finest gardens, villas and vistas can be experienced, while taking in one of the world's greatest city sunsets.

🌑 Customs & Culture

As grand churches and basilicas sprung up during the medieval times, followed by the splendor of the Renaissance, the trend of Florence's aesthetically pleasing culture continues today through some of the world's leading designers like Gucci and Ferragamo. Florence has had style for over 1000 years, and the trendy locals show no sign of changing that any time soon. Stylish boutiques line the city's streets whilst the masterpieces of the past reflect in their windows, while Florentines themselves tend to make an effort when it comes to dressing, especially for formal occasions and dinners, and the dress sense of the locals can be seen on the streets any time of day.

FLORENCE TRAVEL GUIDE

It is not just the appearance that Italians like to keep in check. Most Italians will only drink the odd one or two glasses wine or beer with an evening meal, and excessive drinking – especially over dinner – is rare and highly frowned upon. Like in many parts of Italy, Florentines greet each other with a light embrace and a kiss on each cheek, and it is not uncommon for men to do this when greeting each other.

Florence's culture is however most famous for its artistic heritage. Cimabue and Giotti, the fathers of Italian painting; Donatello, Masacchio, Botticelli, Da Vinci and Michelangelo all lived and worked in Florence, and all contributed to the city's stunning art.

🌐 Geography

Located 129 kilometres (80 miles) from Italy's west coast and the Mediterranean, and 230 kilometres (145 miles) northwest of the capital Rome, Florence's spot on the boot of Italy lies in the heart of Tuscany, the country's most famous region, along the River Arno. Surrounded by a circle of sandstone hills and the Apennine Mountain Range a little further out, Florence is located perfectly for ease of access, and for exploring the nearby cities and regions.

The city itself is divided into numerous neighbourhoods – or areas – which are all jammed close together. Duomo, Piazza del Signoria, San Lorenzo, Piazza Santa Trinita, Santa Maria Novella, San Marco, Santa Croce, Oltrarno make up the different parts of the city, with many of them being createdfor the family rivalries during the Renaissance.

🌍 Weather & Best Time to Visit

With its Mediterranean climate, the city can get hot during the summer months of July and August, with temperatures in the late 30's (°C) not uncommon. July and August are also peak tourist season, as well as vacation time in Italy, meaning just like many parts of the country it is not uncommon to find local shops and businesses closed for a few weeks.

The brief winter In Florence is mild, and can be quite pleasant and crisp, with a few rainy days scheduled each month between November and April. Temperatures do get down to around 1°C (33°F). With the summer months of July and August averaging highs of 30°C (87 °F), the best time of year to visit is during the city's pleasant autumn months of September and October. There is still plenty of sunshine to be had at this time year, however temperatures are a little lower, and more comfortable, and the city is a lot less crowded. Spring (March-May) is also a great time to visit, although there is typically a little more rainfall this time of year in comparison to the autumn.

For up to date weather forecasts for Florence, see:

http://www.theweathernetwork.com/weather/itxx0028

Sights & Activities: What to See & Do

 Accademia Gallery

Originally a 14th century hospital, the Accademia Gallery

opened up as Europe's first Academy of Drawing in 1563,

and is still in operation today. Many of Florence's most

renowned artists including Giorgio Vasari attended the

academy to increase its prestige, and today it is visited by

millions of tourists every year. With numerous works

including Botticelli's world famous Madonna and

Child and Madonna of the Sea, and Giambologna's original plaster copy of the Rape of the Sabines, as well as works by Filippino Lippi, Pontormo, and Bronzino.

While many tourists would happily line up to see the aforementioned works, it is one striking piece of art which makes the Accedemia Gallery the number one place in Florence to visit. After spending almost 400 years outside, Michelangelo's David was moved to the Accademia Gallery in 1873. Sculpted between 1501 and 1504 by a then 26 year old Michelangelo, David is a true masterpiece and confirmed his creator as the most celebrated sculptor of his day.

FLORENCE TRAVEL GUIDE

The statue was originally said to be part of a collection of 12 proposed sculptures from the Old Testament, which were to be placed on the buttresses of the Cathedral of Santa Maria del Fiore. Two of these sculptures had already been completed, Donatello's Joshua, and Agostino'sHercules, both made of Terracotta, and it was actually Agostino who began the original work of David, however he only got as far as roughly shaping the legs before his association with the work was ended for reasons unknown. After 25 years of neglect, the contract was eventually offered to Michelangelo, who began working on the sculpture within a week.

There are many stories and tales of how Michelangelo spent his days planning and executing the transition of a 16ft block of marble into one of the world's most remarkable pieces of art, including how he spent eight hours each day 'staring' at the block for four months, before eventually using his hands. While many stories remain unaccounted for, what is still clear to this day is the masterpiece that this block of marble has become.

With proportions and features clearly indicating that it was designed to be looked at from below, the statue's sheer, imposing size comes as a surprise to many visitors. David was originally placed high on a pedestal outside the Piazza della Signora, which now houses a replica. From here his eyes were said to be gazing towards his opponent Goliath, with his anxious emotion masterfully recreated with the tendons in his neck standing out, his tight upper lip the veins in his lowered right hand bulging out.

While photographs are not allowed, the statue of David is memorable to see in real life, and should top most Florence itineraries regardless of your fondness for art.

Via Ricasoli, 66

50122 Florence, Italy

Tel.: 055 215449

Web: www.accademia.firenze.it/new/ (Italian)

Web: www.florence-museum.com/Accademia

Entrance: €15.25

Opening hours: Tuesday to Sunday: 8:15am to 6:50pm

🌐 Il Duomo & Campanile Bell Tower

One of the most iconic images of Renaissance architecture, Il Duomo and Campanile Bell Tower stand next to each other overlooking the Piazza del Signora, and both offer breathtaking views of the city's terracotta rooftops from their respective lookout points.

The duomo, also known as Basilica Di Sant Maria Del Fiore, has long been the regarded as the heart of the city, both geographically and religiously, and has remained one of the symbolic images of Florence's skyline for over 600 years. Almost 175 years in the making, construction began in September 1296 under the direction of Arnolfo di Cambio, with famous names such as Giotto and Brunelleschi playing a significant role in the design later on. It was officially completed in 1469 when a copper ball crafted by local Florentine sculptor Andrea del Verrocchio was placed at the top of the cathedral's Dome.

For a rewarding 360° panoramic view of the city, a climb of 463 steps is necessary to reach the domes lookout point. From here, a breathtaking view of Florence surrounded by the Tuscan hills can be enjoyed.

While the cathedrals exterior is as breathtaking as any Renaissance building, the huge interior can take a little exploring to unveil the treasures that it holds, due to an empty impression given by many of the rooms and halls. Many of the cathedrals original decorations have been lost over the years, or transferred to the Museum Opera del Duomo.

One of the most breathtaking adornments within the cathedral is on the dome ceiling itself. Giorgio Vasari's fresco of the Last Judgement, which he began in 1572, took seven years to complete. Vasari died before the completion of the work, which was taken over by Federico Zuccari and a number of other collaborators. The crypt of Santa Reparata – the original fifth century church that once stood on the present site -is housed within the cathedral and contains ruins of the church, as well as some Roman remains of the streets that it was built upon.

The Campanile - also known as Giotto's Bell Tower or Campanile di Giotto, was named after its original designer Giotto di Bondone, and stands adjacent to Il Duomo. Built as a bell tower for the cathedral, work began on the

Campanile 40 years after construction had begun on Il Duomo, although the tower was completed 110 years before the cathedrals official completion date. At a height of the 84m (276-ft), the tower was primarily worked on by Giotto until his death in 1337, with only the lower floor completed at this stage. Giotto's successor - Andrea Pisano - diagnosed that the original plans meant the tower had a high risk of collapsing, and went on to doubled the thickness of the tower walls, as well as adding the statues to the tower's exterior. The top three levels were completed by Francesco Talenti, who added numerous windows to atone for the base's perceived density.

The Campanile also offers one of the best lookout points in the city, with a climb of 414 steps required to reach the top. From here one can take an alternative look across the city, with a close up exterior view of the duomo's dome.

Piazza Duomo,

Firenze, 50122

Italy

Tel.: (+39) 055 215380

Web: www.duomofirenze.it

Email: info@duomofirenze.it

Admission to the cathedral is free, while there is an €8 charge to visit the dome and crypt.

Opening hours: Monday, Wednesday and Friday, 10:00am until 5:00pm; Thursday, 10:00am until 3:30pm;

Saturday, 10:00am until 4:45pm; Sunday, 1:30pm until 4:45pm.

🌐 Ponte Vecchio

Meaning 'Old Bridge' in English, the Ponte Vecchio is the oldest of Florence's bridges and today remains one of the most symbolic images of the city. The bridge was originally thought to have been built long before the Renaissance period, with it first appearing in a document in 996, before being badly damaged by severe flooding in 1117.

The bridge was finally rebuilt in 1333 only to be destroyed again the same year, and it wasn't until 1345 when it was completed to its current state as part of the wave of Renaissance construction. The Ponte Vecchio was the only bridge in Florence to survive the attacks during the Second World War, which was said to be an express order by Hitler, who supposedly believed the bridge was too beautiful to blow up.

The bridge is well known for the shops that are stacked along and hang over the edge of the bridge. The shops on the bridge were originally used as workshops, and were also rented by butchers and tanners. In 1593 they were replaced by goldsmiths due to the sheer amount of waste and foul smell caused by the current occupants. Today the premises are favoured by jewelers as well as shoemakers and tourist shops.

One of the most interesting attractions for tourists visiting the Ponte Vecchio and the nearby PlazzadellaSignoria, is the Vasari corridor. Almost a kilometre in length, Giorgio Vasari created the elevated, covered walkway under the instruction of Grand Duke Cosimo I de' Medici in 1564, who wanted to move freely and conveniently between his residence at the Palazzo Pitti on the north side of the Arno River, to the Palazzo Vecchio and the government palace. The walkway begins at the Palazzo Vecchio and joins the Uffizi gallery, before crossing the Ponte Vecchio above the shops. When crossing the bridge, there are numerous panoramic windows looking out onto the River Arno. Whist the walkway is a unique attraction; numerous parts are closed to visitors.

Ponte Vecchio,

50125 Firenze,

Italy

Tel.: (+39) 055 290 832

☻ Uffizi Gallery

One of the oldest museums in the western world, the Uffizi - which means 'offices' – was originally built as offices for the Florentine magistrates, and is now one of the most visited museums in the world. The gallery is housed in the building designed by Vasari in 1560, and built by Cosimo I of Medici. The collection began in 1574 by Cosimo's son, Francesco I, who converted the second floor into a place where he was said to have wanted 'to walk in with paintings, sculptures and other precious things'.

FLORENCE TRAVEL GUIDE

The sheer collection housed at the Uffizi – said to be only masterpieces – is regarded by many as incomparable to any other collection in the world, and features a plethora of works from some of the world's most renowned artists, including Leonardo da Vinci, Sandro Botticelli, Giotto, Michelangelo, Raphael, Cimabue and many more.

Via della Ninna, 5,

50122 Firenze, Italy

Tel.: (+39) 055 238 8651

Web: www.uffizi.firenze.it

Admission is €8.50, cash only.

Opening hours: Tuesday to Sunday, 8:15am until 6:50pm.

🌎 Piazza della Signoria

Adorned with 16th century statues, fountains, and classic

Renaissance architecture, The Piazza della Signoria has

remained the center of political life in the city for almost

700 years, and is dominated by the striking Palazzo

Vecchio which overlooks the L shaped plaza. It was here

were many spectacles of great triumph were seen, such

as the much celebrated return of the Medici in 1530.

Today the square is still seen as the ideal meeting place

for local Florentines and tourists alike, due to its ideal

location close to the Ponte Vecchio bridge and Arno

River, the Duomo, and the Uffizi.

The many sculptures in Piazza della Signoria are

associated with past political undertones, including

Michelangelo's David, which has since been moved to

the Galleria dell'Accademia and replaced with a replica.

Originally standing tall outside the Palazzo Vecchio, David

was seen as an indication of Florence's bold opposition of

the later, more ruthless Medici, while Bandinelli's Hercules

and Cacus, now standing to the right of David's replica,

was appointed by the Medici to display their physical

power after their return from displacement.

The building on the corner of the square is the Loggia dei

Lanzi, also known as the Loggia della Signoria, and is

effectively an open-air sculpture gallery of Renaissance

art. Featuring three huge arches which are open to the

rest of the square, the building features Cellini's 1554

statue of Perseo holding the head of Medusa, which took

ten years in the making and was seen as a blunt reminder

of the consequences of opposing the Medici.

FLORENCE TRAVEL GUIDE

Giambologna's Rape of the Sabines, is also featured amongst many other beautiful sculptures found beneath the arches of the Loggia dei Lanzi.

Many tourists can spend a long afternoon here people watching while enjoying an Italian latte or an offering from one of the nearby gelato stores, and there are also numerous restaurants around the square with great outdoor dining areas, for breakfast, lunch, or a formal dinner.

Piazza della Signoria, 5,

50122 Firenze

Web: www.piazza-signoria.com

🌑 Castello del Trebbio

When touring around Florence, gawping at the city's architectural splendours and being surrounded by tourists from all over the world, it is easy to forget that you are in Tuscany – the Tuscany of endless, rolling hills dotted with typical Italian villas and penetrated by slim country roads. The good news is that the quintessential Tuscany experience many dream about is only a 30 minute drive away from the city, and can be had at Castello del Trebbio, a 12th century castle which housed both the Pazzi and Medici families, and now offers an unforgettable experience in the heart of the fairy tale Tuscan countryside.

Originallybuilt as a fortress in the twelfth century for the Pazzi family, the castles proprietary was taken over by the

Medici family who proceeded to turn the fortress into a luxury villa.

Today, the castle is surrounded by olive groves – with over 10,000 olive trees - and grape vines and has been fully restored to its original state, with the current owners having respected its long history.

Tourists either visit for the day to explore the wine cellars, and to sample the top quality olive oil along with the cheese and meat platters the castle offers. Wine tours are also very common; however most visits are by tourists looking to spend time relaxing in Tuscan countryside in one of the castles apartments or villas. There is also pasta making classes, a fantastic restaurant and outdoor swimming pool.

Via Santa Brigida, 9

50060 Santa Brigida (Florence)

Italy

(+39) 055 830 4900

http://www.vinoturismo.it/

Price for stays less than seven days: €50 per person per night, with reduced prices for children under 12 years of age. There is a minimum stay of two nights. Apartments need to be booked for at least one week.

The Medici Villas

Said to be the godfathers of the Renaissance, the Medici were a powerful family who rose from a small Italian community to amass unparalleled wealth, spearhead the

Renaissance, and rule Europe for over 300 years. With a huge interest in education, they pushed for a rebirth in all forms, and were not afraid to spend in order to encourage a new world approach to learning.

This resulted in a lot of investment from the family in the cities artistic heritage, which to this day has resulted in Florence being regarded as one of the world's most beautiful.

The Medici family owned numerous rural building complexes around the outskirts of Florence, which they used for recreation and holidays. Although all contrasting, the villas are known for their pristine gardens, classic architecture and interiors littered with artistic masterpieces from paintings and sculptures to antique furniture and adorning frescos.

FLORENCE TRAVEL GUIDE

The Medici Villa in Poggio a Caiano is straight forward to reach by public transport, while Florence Tour offer guided tours of a selection of the villas. See www.florencetour.com for more information.

The Medici Villa

Piazza de Medici 14,

59016 Poggio a Caiano

Tel.: (+39) 055 238 8796

Admission to the villa is free year round.

Opening hours: 8:15am until 6:30pm, with closing times depending on the season

A local bus service can take tourists to the gates of the villa, which depart from Via Nazionale near the train station. Take a bus leaving for either Poggio a Caiano, Pistoia or Quarrata, all three will stop directly in front of the villa.

Piazzale Michelangelo

A popular spot for a relaxing afternoon, Piazzale Michelangelo offers some of the best panoramic views of the city and its surrounding valley, and is a popular sunset spot for locals and tourists alike. The Piazza was designed in 1869 by local architect Giuseppe Poggi. He wanted to create a monument base for where Michelangelo's work could be displayed to the public.

While Poggi's vision was never realized – the intended building that was built to be the museum is now a restaurant – the piazza has become a major tourist spot in modern day Florence, primarily for its views. The piazza is filled with tourists and vendors, as well as a bronze replica of Michelangelo's David. The piazza can easily be reached by taking the number 12 or 13 bus from the center, while the double decker sightseeing buses also stop at the piazza. For the more adventurous, climbing up from Piazza Poggi – which sits at the base of the hill - will lead you to Piazzale Michelangelo.

It is important to remember that while most of the piazza is now a car park, there are limited things to do once at the top of the hill. The view alone is the prime reason many people like to spend an afternoon relaxing here.

Piazzale Michelangelo

50125 Firenze,

Italy

Tel.: (+39) 055 055

🌐 Boboli Garden & Pitti Palace

The Boboli Garden and its surrounding areas were

created by the Medici in 1549 when Eleonora di Toledo -

the wife of Duke Cosimo I - purchased the Palazzo Pitti.

Cosimo I recruited the most renowned landscape

gardeners of his time to lay out the expansive garden as a

backdrop to their new palace where they resided. The

garden also hosts to a fantastic collection of statues and

fountains.

Over the years the garden was expanded many times as more and more statues and fountains were added, before the garden was opened to the public in 1776. From the top of the terraces you can find remarkable vistas of Florence and the surrounding Arno Valley. There is an amphitheater within the Boboli Garden situated just behind the Pitti Palace, and this and was once the location of the quarry that gave the palace its stone.

Palazzo Pitti,

Piazza dèPitti, 1,

50125 Firenze,

Italy

Tel.: (+39) 055 229 8732

Web: www.giardinodiboboli.it

Hours: Daily, 8:15am until 4:30pm (November February); 8:15am until 5:30pm (March); 8:15am until 6:30pm (April, May, September and October; 8:15am until 5:30pm (October when Daylight Saving Time ends); 8:15am until 7:30pm (June and August). Entry is permitted up to an hour before closing time.

Cost: Adults and all non-EU, €7; EU citizens aged 18 to 25, €3.50; EU citizens aged below 18 or older than 65, FREE. ID is required for EU citizens.

🌐 Basilica di San Miniato al Monte

Just a five minute walk from the Piazzale Michelangelo is the San Miniato al Monte church – meaning St. Minias on the Hill - one of Tuscany's most original and bona fide

Romanesque churches. Designed by Giuseppe Poggi, the church is surrounded by a series of stairs and terraces, and built between 1865 and 1873. Like the aforementioned surrounding places, the area also offers a spectacular view of the city and is usually explored in conjunction with the Piazzale Michelangelo.

The church has its own interesting history, and was built above the grave of Saint Minias. He was decapitated and buried at the top of the hill, with the church being built shortly after he was buried. The façade was created in 1090, and has an elegant, green and white marble coloured decoration. The basilica also houses a partially finished campanile, which was created in 1523, replacing an older tower that had collapsed in 1499. The current bell tower was used to defend the city during the siege of

Florence in 1529 and 1530, by the then ousted Medici

and their followers.

Via Monte alle Croci,

Firenze,

Italy.

(+39) 055 234 2731

www.san-miniato-al-monte.com

Budget Tips

 Accommodation

While Florence has never, and probably will never be

regarded as a cheap getaway, there are certainly options

dotted all around the city for inexpensive places to stay

and eat, by western European standards. The best rates

for hostels and Bed and Breakfasts can be found between

September and April, while most hotels have special

offers on outside of the summer season.

Accommodations and restaurants with the lowest prices

are typically located a little outside of the tourist meccas

of Plaza del Signoria and other notable points of interest

in the city centre, and sometimes just a ten or fifteen

minute walk away from the main squares and attractions

can yield more reasonable prices for the budget traveller.

🌐 Hotel Sampaoli

Via San Gallo, 14

50129 Firenze,

Italy

Tel.: (+39) 055 284 834

Web: http://www.hotelsampaoli.it/

FLORENCE TRAVEL GUIDE

Rates: €29-€32.50 per person per night for a private double or twin room with a shared bathroom (+€5 per person per night for en-suite bathroom.) The hotel also offers private three bed (€27), four bed (€23), and five bed (€19) rooms, all with private en-suite bathrooms, and all prices quoted per person per night.

Situated within a 1000 year old building, and in the heart of Florence, the Hotel Sampaoli offers guests a quiet and simple stay, while being just minutes away from the all of the major attraction and transportation hubs offered by the city. The Santa Maria Novella train station, which connects Florence the rest of Italy, is just minutes away, while a short walk in the opposite direction will lead you to the Duomo and the Accademia Gallery.

All rooms offer a TV with DCD player, and all have access to the hotels free Wi-Fi, and the welcoming atmosphere provided by the staff will help ensure a pleasant stay in the city of art.

Garibaldi's Relais & Charme

Via Pratese 34,

Florence,

Italy

Tel.: (+39) 055 342 4625

Web: http://relaisgaribaldis.wordpress.com/

Rates: €12-€14 for a mixed or female only dorm; €38.50 per person per night in a private twin or double room.

FLORENCE TRAVEL GUIDE

Located just ten minutes away from the city centre in a peaceful, residential area of Florence, Garibaldi Relais is a family run villa set within the lush greenery of its own private garden, and offers both business and leisure travelers a relaxing retreat away from the hustle and bustle of the city centre. The guest rooms are decorated in a classic style, with Wi-Fi access, tea and coffee making facilities, and fresh linens, while the villa also has a computer station located in the lobby.

Additionally facilities include the offer of free parking, bicycle hire, an on-site café, an outdoor terrace and free city maps. GarbaldiRelais is located just minutes away from the main railway station, the business district and the Roberto Cavalli shopping outlet for those looking for some retail therapy.

Hostel Greci

Borgodei Greci 13, Florence, Italy

Tel:(+39) 349 360 0709

Web: http://www.hostelgreci.hostel.com/

Rates: €59 per person per night for a double or twin room with a private en-suite bathroom. €49 for a female only, two bed dorm.

For those wanting to be in the heart of the action at the best possible price, the Hostel Greci is located in the heart Florence, and is a short walk from all of the city centre's major attractions, being just one minute from the Uffizi, Plaza dellaSignoria and the Ponte Vecchio.

The hostel offers a warm ambience, with a common room, 24 hour security, tours desk and luggage storage, while all rooms come with fresh linens and a reading light.

David Inn

Via Ricasoli 31

Firenze, Italy

Tel: (+39) 055 213 707

Web: http://www.davidinn.hostel.com/

Rates: €25-€27 per person per night in a four bed mixed dorm.

Another property in the heart of Florence, the David Inn is located just one block away from its namesake and most famous David in the city, Michelangelo's David, housed inside the Accedemia Gallery. The hostel also has views of the nearby Duomo. The hostel has gained a reputation for its cleanliness, and its bright, airy, and quiet rooms.

Major facilities include a common room, free internet access, luggage storage, personal lockers, free city maps from the tours desk and cable TV, while all rooms come equipped with individual reading lights, hot showers, and linens.

Soggiorno Pitti

Palazzo Pitti, 8

50125 Firenze,

Italy

Tel.: (+39) 055 392 1483

Web: www.soggiornopitti.com

FLORENCE TRAVEL GUIDE

Rates: €33-€38 for a single room, €23.50 per person per night for a twin or double (shared bathroom) and €30 for a twin or double with a private en-suite bathroom.

The mixed dorm is €16 per person per night, while the hostel also offers private three bed (€25) and four bed (€22) rooms both with a private en-suite bathroom.

Housed in an early twentieth-century building on the north side of the Arno River, and within the historic center of Florence, the SoggiornoPitti is situated just in front of Pitti Palace and offers convenient access to the nearby sites or to the Ponte Vecchio where you can cross and be in the Plaza dellaSignoria within minutes.

Facilities include a large, free breakfast, common room, internet access, café, luggage storage and tours desk.

Places to Eat

Florence as a whole is consistently held in the upper echelons of city's which have a remarkable and outstanding food options, and this catering isn't just reserved for the fancy, overpriced restaurants aimed at free spending tourists. There are a plethora of options available ranging from sit down restaurants, hole-in-the-wall eateries and a wealth of quick fix dessert options for those with a sweet tooth.

Le Campane

Borgo La Croce 85/87.

50124 Firenze, Italy

Tel.: (+39) 55-23-41-101

Web: www.le-campane.it

Price: between €8 and €11 per person for dinner.

After undergoing a major facelift in 2006, Le Campane is a classic Italian Pizzeria, and offers two air conditioned rooms with great wall art and images for those wanting to dine in, while also offering a reasonable take out menu for those wanting to take some fresh pizza back to their lodgings. There is also an outside dining area.

The restaurant offers a full lunch and dinner menu at rock bottom prices in comparison to many city centre restaurants in Florence, although it is best known for its pizzas. The Margherita and Neopolitan pizzas are very

well received, and both highly recommended.

IL GIOVA

Via Borgo

La Croce, 73

Firenze, Italy

Tel.: (+39) 055 248 0639

Web: www.ilgiova.com

Price: From €11 per person.

Possibly one of the smallest restaurants in the city, this is

a great family run restaurant offering freshly made bread,

pasta and sauces, and excellent service to boot. Located

a little walk from the centre of Florence, on the east side

in the La Croce area, Il Giova is slowly becoming one of

the city's worst kept secrets, and reservations are recommended for dinner.

Highly recommended is the filet mignon, or the pork fillet with caramelized onions, while the chocolate cake for dessert has earned rave reviews.

Il Pizza Iuolo

Via dèMacci, 113

50122 Firenze,

Italy

Tel.: (+39) 055 241 171

Web: www.ilpizzaiuolo.it

Price: €8-€22 per person for dinner.

A bustling restaurant located in the centre of Florence, IlPizzaiuolo offers some of the best appetizers in the city, with the house appetizer changing regularly. Neopolitan thick crust pizza is a highlight from the pizza menu, while the spaghetti al vongole is well received from the mains menu. The restaurant is extremely popular amongst both local Florentine's and tourists alike, and this shows in the warm, bubbly atmosphere that hits you when you walk into the place. Because of its popularity, reservations are highly recommended to avoid the long wait time, or going outside of the prime time hours (7:30pm to 9:30pm).

Grom

Via delle Oche,

50122 Firenze,

Italy

Tel.: (+39) 055 216 158

Web:www.grom.it

Price: €3-€6

With stores throughout Italy, Grom is held in high regard for its Gelato, which come in many different choices and included a variety of chocolates. Although it can be tricky to find - situated down a narrow side street - there is normally a line up at the store, paying testament to wealth of positive reviews and hype this gelateria has gained. Being just metres away from the Duomo, Grom is a perfect pit stop for the inevitable, late night Italian Gelato experience.

Blue River

Lungarno Delle Grazie 12,

Florence, Italy

Price: €7.50 meals. Desserts: From €3

A small hole-in-the-wall restaurant located between the Uffizi and the Bibliotecha, the Blue River offers a drink, a large salad and main course for just €7.50, and is an ideal choice for tourists on a budget. The restaurant is also popular with local Florentine's who chat to the owner over home pressed coffee while he tends to the line of customers.

With some fantastic desserts and sweets also available, the Blue River is perfect for grabbing a filling lunch or just a quick stop-gap.

🌐 Shopping

Whether you are in the market for some leather goods, gold, or just some good old retail therapy, Florence, like all major Italian cities can offer some of the world's biggest names.

While the top end designers like Gucci, Ferragamo, Pucci, and Armani are all located around the streets of the streets of Via Tornabuoni, Via dellaVignaNuova, and Via deiCalzaiuol, there are also options that won't break the bank, and will ensure some memorabilia from your Florence trip.

Stockhouse Il Giglio

Borgo Ognissanti 64

50123 Firenze

For those interested in the fashion labels, but not too keen on the price nor the season, pay a visit to the Stockhouse Giglio sells 'last year's trends' – a big no-no for fashion followers, yet hardly a problem for the majority of shoppers - at a fraction of their original prices, due to the inability to shift these in the original stores. While some clothes can hold their prices, it is definitely worth a visit as both men and women's designer clothing can be found for a great bargain.

Farmacia del Mercato Centrale

Via dell'Ariento, 87-r

50123 Firenze

A must for food fanatics, the Farmacia del Mercato

Centrale offers some of the freshest produce in the city at reasonably low prices. Known for its fantastic choice of great meat, bread and cheese, the store is also popular – and highly recommended – for those staying in Florence longer than a few days and who would like to pick up some local produce to cook at their apartment.

Trade here has been in operation for over 100 years, with some of the original signage and jars still on display.

Monaco Metropolitano

Via Ramaglianti, 6/R

50125 Firenze

Tel.: (+39) 055 268 121

Web: www.monacometropolitano.com

Email: monacometropolitano@gmail.co

For those in the hunt for leather, all offerings might seem the same when browsing the many outlets in Florence. This is where Monaco Metropolitano is different. Located on the north side of the Arno River, in the district known as Oltarno, it is just a few minutes' walk from the Ponte Vecchio, and offers a remarkable collection of handmade leather products, which are created daily by the skilled staff using original methods and tools combined with modern ideas.

New ideas and designs are born every day, and one can watch the skilled old timers or enthusiastic students show you the process of making such products by hand.

Know Before You Go

🌐 Entry Requirements

By virtue of the Schengen agreement, travellers from other countries in the European Union do not need a visa when visiting Italy. Additionally Swiss travellers are also exempt. Visitors from certain other countries such as the USA, Canada, Japan, Israel, Australia and New Zealand do not need visas if their stay in Italy does not exceed 90 days. When entering Italy you will be required to make a declaration of presence, either at the airport, or at a police station within eight days of arrival. This applies to visitors from other Schengen countries, as well as those visiting from non-Schengen countries.

🌐 Health Insurance

Citizens of other EU countries are covered for emergency health care in Italy. UK residents, as well as visitors from Switzerland are covered by the European Health Insurance Card (EHIC), which can be applied for free of charge. Visitors from non-Schengen countries will need to show proof of private health insurance that is valid for the duration of their stay in Italy (that offers at least €37,500 coverage), as part of their visa application. No special vaccinations are required.

🌐 Travelling with Pets

Italy participates in the Pet Travel Scheme (PETS) which allows UK residents to travel with their pets without requiring quarantine upon re-entry. Certain conditions will need to be met. The animal will have to be microchipped and up to date on rabies vaccinations. In the case of dogs, a vaccination against canine distemper is also required by the Italian authorities. When travelling from the USA, your pet will need to be micro-chipped or marked with an identifying tattoo and up to date on rabies vaccinations. An EU Annex IV Veterinary Certificate for Italy will need to be issued by an accredited veterinarian. On arrival in Italy, you can apply for an EU pet passport to ease your travel in other EU countries.

🌐 Airports

Fiumicino – Leonardo da Vinci International Airport (FCO) is one of the busiest airports in Europe and the main international airport of Italy. It is located about 35km southwest of the historical quarter of Rome. Terminal 5 is used for trans-Atlantic and international flights, while Terminals 1, 2 and 3 serve mainly for domestic flights and medium haul flights to other European destinations. Before Leonardo da Vinci replaced it, the **Ciampino–G. B. Pastine International Airport** (CIA) was the main international airport servicing Rome and Italy. It is one of the oldest airports in the country still in use. Although it declined in importance, budget airlines such as Ryanair boosted its air traffic in recent years. The airport is used by Wizz Air, V Bird, Helvetic, Transavia Airlines, Sterling, Ryanair, Thomsonfly, EasyJet, Air Berlin, Hapag-Lloyd Express and Carpatair.

Milan Malpensa Airport (MXP) is the largest of the three airports serving the city of Milan. Located about 40km northwest of Milan's city center, it connects travellers to the regions of Lombardy, Piedmont and Liguria. **Milan Linate Airport** (LIN) is Milan's second international airport. **Venice Marco Polo Airport** (VCE) provides access to the charms of Venice. **Olbia Costa Smeralda Airport** (OLB) is located near Olbia, Sardinia. Main regional airports are **Guglielmo Marconi Airport** (BLQ), an international airport servicing the region of Bologna, **Capodichino Airport** at Naples (NAP), **Pisa International Airport** (PSA), formerly Galileo Galilei Airport, the main airport serving Tuscany, **Sandro Pertini Airport** near Turin (TRN), **Cristoforo Colombo** in Genoa (GOA), **Punta Raisi Airport** in Palermo (PMO), **Vincenzo Bellini Airport** in Catania (CTA) and **Palese Airport** in Bari (BRI).

🌏 Airlines

Alitalia is the flag carrier and national airline of Italy. It has a subsidiary, Alitalia CityLiner, which operates short-haul regional flights. Air Dolomiti is a regional Italian based subsidiary of of the Lufthansa Group. Meridiana is a privately owned airline based at Olbia in Sardinia.

Fiumicino - Leonardo da Vinci International Airport serves as the main hub for Alitalia, which has secondary hubs at Milan Linate and Milan Malpensa Airport. Alitalia CityLiner uses Fiumicino – Leonardo da Vinci International Airport as main hub and has secondary hubs at Milan-Linate, Naples and Trieste. Fiumicino – Leonardo da Vinci International Airport is also one of two primary hubs used by the budget Spanish airline Vueling. Milan Malpensa Airport is one of the largest bases for the British budget airline EasyJet. Venice Airport serves as an Italian base for the Spanish budget airline, Volotea, which provides connections mainly to other destinations in Europe. Olbia Costa Smeralda Airport (OLB), located near Olbia, Sardinia is the primary base of Meridiana, a private Italian Airline in partnership with Air Italia and Fly Egypt.

Currency

Italy's currency is the Euro. It is issued in notes in denominations of €500, €200, €100, €50, €20, €10 and €5. Coins are issued in denominations of €2, €1, 50c, 20c, 10c, 5c, 2c and 1c.

Banking & ATMs

Using ATMs or Bancomats, as they are known in Italy, to withdraw money is simple if your ATM card is compatible with the MasterCard/Cirrus or Visa/Plus networks. There is a €250 limit on daily withdrawals. Italian machines are configured for 4-digit PIN numbers, although some machines will be able to handle longer PIN numbers. Bear in mind some Bancomats can run out of cash over weekends and that the more remote villages may not have adequate banking facilities so plan ahead.

Credit Cards

Credit cards are valid tender in most Italian businesses. While Visa and MasterCard are accepted universally, most tourist oriented businesses also accept American Express and Diners Club. Credit cards issued in Europe are smart cards that that are fitted with a microchip and require a PIN for each transaction.

This means that a few ticket machines, self-service vendors and other businesses may not be configured to accept the older magnetic strip credit cards. Do remember to advise your bank or credit card company of your travel plans before leaving.

🌍 Tourist Taxes

Tourist tax varies from city to city, as each municipality sets its own rate. The money is collected by your accommodation and depends on the standard of accommodation. A five star establishment will levy a higher amount than a four star or three star establishment. You can expect to pay somewhere between €1 and €7 per night, with popular destinations like Rome, Venice, Milan and Florence charging a higher overall rate. In some regions, the rate is also adjusted seasonally. Children are usually exempt until at least the age of 10 and sometimes up to the age of 18. In certain areas, disabled persons and their companions also qualify for discounted rates. Tourist tax is payable directly to the hotel or guesthouse before the end of your stay.

🌍 Reclaiming VAT

If you are not from the European Union, you can claim back VAT (Value Added Tax) paid on your purchases in Italy. The

VAT rate in Italy is 21 percent and this can be claimed back on your purchases if certain conditions are met. The merchant needs to be partnered with a VAT refund program. This will be indicated if the shop displays a "Tax Free" sign. The shop assistant will fill out a form for reclaiming VAT. When you submit this at the airport, you will receive your refund.

🌐 Tipping Policy

If your bill includes the phrase "coperto e servizio", that means that a service charge or tip is already included. Most waiting staff in Italy are salaried workers, but if the service is excellent, a few euros extra would be appreciated.

🌐 Mobile Phones

Most EU countries, including Italy use the GSM mobile service. This means that most UK phones and some US and Canadian phones and mobile devices will work in Italy. While you could check with your service provider about coverage before you leave, using your own service in roaming mode will involve additional costs. The alternative is to purchase an Italian SIM card to use during your stay in Italy.

Italy has four mobile networks. They are TIM, Wind, Vodafone and Tre (3) and they all provide pre-paid services. TIM offers two tourist options, both priced at €20 (+ €10 for the SIM card) with a choice of two packages - 2Gb data, plus 200 minutes call time or internet access only with a data allowance of 5Gb. Vodafone, Italy's second largest network offers a Vodafone Holiday package including SIM card for €30. They also offer the cheapest roaming rates. Wind offers an Italian Tourist pass for €20 which includes 100 minutes call time and 2Gb data and can be extended with a restart option for an extra €10.

To purchase a local SIM card, you will need to show your passport or some other form of identification and provide your residential details in Italy. By law, SIM registration is required prior to activation. Most Italian SIM cards expire after a 90 day period of inactivity. When dialling internationally, remember to use the (+) sign and the code of the country you are connecting to.

Dialling Code

The international dialling code for Italy is +39.

Emergency Numbers

Police: 113

Fire: 115

Ambulance: 118

MasterCard: 800 789 525

Visa: 800 819 014

🌍 Public Holidays

1 January: New Year's Day (Capodanno)

6 January: Day of the Epiphany (Epifania)

March-April: Easter Monday (Lunedì dell'Angelo or Pasquetta)

25 April: Liberation Day (Festa della Liberazione)

1 May: International Worker's Day (Festa del Lavoro / Festa dei Lavoratori)

2 June: Republic Day (Festa della Repubblica)

15 August: Assumption Day (Ferragosto / Assunta)

1 November: All Saints Day (Tutti i santi / Ognissanti)

8 December: Immaculate Conception (Immacolata Concezione / Immacolata)

25 December: Christmas Day (Natale)

26 December: St Stephen's Day (Santo Stefano)

A number of Saints days are observed regionally throughout the year.

🌍 Time Zone

Italy falls in the Central European Time Zone. This can be calculated as Greenwich Mean Time/Coordinated Universal

Time (GMT/UTC) +2; Eastern Standard Time (North America) -6; Pacific Standard Time (North America) -9.

🌎 Daylight Savings Time

Clocks are set forward one hour on 29 March and set back one hour on 25 October for Daylight Savings Time.

🌎 School Holidays

The academic year begins in mid September and ends in mid June. The summer holiday is from mid June to mid September, although the exact times may vary according to region. There are short breaks around Christmas and New Year and also during Easter. Some regions such as Venice and Trentino have an additional break during February for the carnival season.

🌎 Trading Hours

Trading hours for the majority of shops are from 9am to 12.30pm and then again from 3.30pm to 7.30pm, although in some areas, the second shift may be from 4pm to 8pm instead. The period between 1pm and 4pm is known in Italy as the *riposo*. Large department shops and malls tend to be open from 9am to 9pm, from Monday to Saturday. Post offices are open from 8.30am to 1.30pm from Monday to Saturday. Most shops and many restaurants are closed on Sundays. Banking hours are from 8.30am to 1.30pm and then again from 3pm to 4pm, Monday to Friday. Most restaurants are open from noon till 2.30pm and then again from 7pm till 11pm or midnight, depending on the establishment. Nightclubs open around 10pm, but only liven up after midnight. Closing times vary, but will generally be between 2am and 4am. Museum hours vary, although major sights tend to be open continuously and often up to 7.30pm. Many museums are closed on Mondays.

🌐 Driving Laws

The Italians drive on the right hand side of the road. A driver's licence from any of the European Union member countries is valid in Italy. Visitors from non-EU countries will require an International Driving Permit that must remain current throughout the duration of their stay in Italy.

The speed limit on Italy's autostrade is 130km per hour and 110km per hour on main extra-urban roads, but this is reduced by 20km to 110km and 90km respectively in rainy weather. On secondary extra-urban roads, the speed limit is 90km per hour; on urban highways, it is 70km per hour and on urban roads, the speed limit is 50km per hour. You are not allowed to drive in the ZTL or Limited Traffic Zone (or *zona traffico limitato* in Italian) unless you have a special permit.

Visitors to Italy are allowed to drive their own non-Italian vehicles in the country for a period of up to six months. After this, they will be required to obtain Italian registration with Italian licence plates. Italy has very strict laws against driving under the influence of alcohol. The blood alcohol limit is 0.05 and drivers caught above the limit face penalties such as fines of up to €6000, confiscation of their vehicles, suspension of their licenses and imprisonment of up to 6 months. Breathalyzer tests are routine at accident scenes.

🌐 Drinking Laws

The legal drinking age in Italy is 16. While drinking in public spaces is allowed, public drunkenness is not tolerated. Alcohol is sold in bars, wine shops, liquor stores and grocery shops.

🌐 Smoking Laws

In 2005, Italy implemented a policy banning smoking from public places such as bars, restaurants, nightclubs and working places, limiting it to specially designated smoking rooms. Further legislation banning smoking from parks, beaches and stadiums is being explored.

🌐 Electricity

Electricity: 220 volts

Frequency: 50 Hz

Italian electricity sockets are compatible with the Type L plugs, a plug that features three round pins or prongs, arranged in a straight line. An alternate is the two-pronged Type C Euro adaptor. If travelling from the USA, you will need a power converter or transformer to convert the voltage from 220 to 110, to avoid damage to your appliances. The latest models of many laptops, camcorders, mobile phones and digital cameras are dual-voltage with a built in converter.

🌐 Tourist Information (TI)

There are tourist information (TI) desks at each of the terminals of the Leonardo da Vinci International Airport, as well as interactive Information kiosks with the latest touch-screen technology. In Rome, the tourist office can be found at 5 Via Parigi, near the Termini Station and it is identified as APT, which stands for Azienda provinciale del Turismo. Free maps and brochures of current events are available from tourist kiosks.

Several of the more tourist-oriented regions of Italy offer tourist cards that include admission to most of the city's attractions.

While these cards are not free, some offer great value for money. A variety of tourism apps are also available online.

🌐 Food & Drink

Pasta is a central element of many typically Italian dishes, but there are regional varieties and different types of pasta are matched to different sauces. Well known pasta dishes such as lasagne and bolognaise originated in Bologna. Stuffed pasta is popular in the northern part of Italy, while the abundance of seafood and olives influences southern Italian cuisine. As far as pizza goes, the Italians differentiate between the thicker Neapolitan pizza and the thin crust Roman pizza, as well as white pizza, also known as focaccia and tomato based pizza. Other standards include minestrone soup, risotto, polenta and a variety of cheeses, hams, sausages and salamis. If you are on a budget, consider snacking on stuzzichini with a few drinks during happy hour which is often between 7 and 9pm. The fare can include salami, cheeses, cured meat, mini pizzas, bread, vegetables, pastries or pate. In Italy, Parmesan refers only to cheese originating from the area surrounding Parma. Favorites desserts include tiramisu or Italian gelato.

Italians enjoy relaxing to aperitifs before they settle down to a meal and their favorites are Campari, Aperol or Negroni, the famous Italian cocktail. Wine is enjoyed with dinner. Italy is particularly famous for its red wines. The best known wine regions are Piedmont, which produces robust and dry reds, Tuscany and Alto Adige, where Alpine soil adds a distinctive acidity. After the meal, they settle down to a glass of limoncello, the country's most popular liqueur, or grappa, which is distilled from grape seeds and stems, as digestive. Other options in this class include a nut liqueur, nocino, strawberry based Fragolino Veneto or herbal digestives like gineprino, laurino or mirto. Italians are also fond of coffee. Espresso is drunk through throughout the day, but cappuccino is considered a morning drink. The most popular beers in Italy are Peroni and Moretti.

 Websites

http://vistoperitalia.esteri.it/home/en
This is the website of the Consulate General of Italy. Here you can look up whether you will need a visa and also process your application online.
http://www.italia.it/en/home.html
The official website of Italian tourism
http://www.italia.it/en/useful-info/mobile-apps.html
Select the region of your choice to download a useful mobile app to your phone.
http://www.italylogue.com/tourism

http://italiantourism.com/index.html

http://www.reidsitaly.com/

http://wikitravel.org/en/Italy

https://www.summerinitaly.com/

http://www.accessibleitalianholiday.com/

Planning Italian vacations around the needs of disabled tourists.